God Did
TOO Make
Adam and Steve

By
Denny Smith

Neil,

what a joy to have
you in class. Life is Good

Denny S.

TABLE OF CONTENTS

ACKNOWLEDGEMENTS

There are so many people to acknowledge for their contributions to this book but I wish to specifically thank Susan Montag, our publishing consultant; Erin Bloch, a counselor at our school for her input and encouragement; Jodee Esser our proof reader and grammar coach; the staff at Sunray Printing Solutions, Inc.; the late Reverend Marcella Lundgren, who started me on a spiritual path to replace judgement with acceptance; our good friends, Joan and Paul Lerdal, for their assistance and optimistic outlook; and to my family for all of their love and support. You will meet them on the dedication page.

CHAPTER ONE

The Sign

The Sign

It was a sign at an anti-gay rally.

The cutting remarks of the participants were filled with anger and hatred as they used biblical references to justify their disdain for gay people. The sign that caught my attention was the one that read: "God made Adam and Eve, not Adam and Steve." I silently asked the question of the holder of the placard, "Well, who *did* make Adam and Steve then? Somebody created them and if there is only One Creator, it must be the same One that created you." At that moment, the purpose for and title of *God Did TOO Make Adam and Steve* came to mind.

The Purpose

Socrates once said, "I cannot teach a person anything. I can only make them think." So it is with the purpose of this book. I cannot, nor do I intend to, change your mind. I only want you to think.

So as you read, momentarily put aside your emotions and think. *Just think.* Think about your own sexual orientation and your choice to be either heterosexual or homosexual. *When did you make the choice to be "gay" or "straight?"* *How* did you make the choice? How did you *learn* to be gay or straight? Who *taught* you how to choose your sexual orientation? If your answer is, "Well, silly, I didn't learn any of these things; they just came *naturally,*" the book has already served its purpose, provided that you realize that a gay person's sexuality came in the same way yours did to you – *naturally.* And if you realize that the One Being who determined your sexual orientation is the same One who determined *everyone's* sexual orientation, including Adam's and Steve's, you are on your way to accepting and loving people regardless of their "gayness" or "straightness."

God Did TOO Make Adam and Steve is written for gay women and men, parents and families of gay women and men, those who accept and love gays, those who hate gay people, and everyone in between. It is written to foster more understanding and acceptance of people, regardless of their sexual orientation. (Perhaps first will come tolerance, then acceptance, then the ultimate – irrelevance.)

14

A Revelation

I was sitting in the church pew waiting for the service to begin – a memorial service for my brother-in-law's life partner. We didn't know they were gay until Rome was diagnosed with a terminal illness. After the service, we gathered back at the house with many of the couple's friends. Their friends couldn't believe the love and support Paul received from his family. Some of them had been ostracized by their families and they admired the unconditional love and total acceptance that existed in ours. Love and acceptance seemed like the natural order of things to us and we were flabbergasted to hear that others had been disowned by their own mothers, fathers, sisters and brothers just because they were gay.

Let's return to my thoughts as I sat in church. I totally accepted their homosexual relationship but didn't understand much about it – that is until I read a note that Rome had written to Paul about their love for each other. It was then I realized that their relationship was no different than the relationship between my wife and me. Theirs was a commitment to a lifetime of love, just like ours. Theirs was a commitment of fidelity, just like ours. Theirs was a commitment to walk through the peaks and valleys together, just like ours. Theirs was a relationship that included sex, but one that went far beyond the bedroom, just like ours.

As time passed, I began to wonder how some

people could be so cruel to others just because of their sexual orientation. As I read the blistering letters to the editors in the newspapers, especially from "religious" people, I wondered how they could be so judgmental and full of hatred towards fellow human beings just because they were gay. Why are some people so willing and even anxious to chastise and demean others; to rip at the very heart of their being? Maybe it's just a lack of understanding, or maybe it's fear. I hope so.

"I CANNOT TEACH A PERSON ANYTHING. I CAN ONLY MAKE THEM THINK."

SOCRATES

Chapter Two

First Acceptance, Then Tolerance, Then Irrelevance

First Acceptance, Then Tolerance, Then Irrelevance

I was watching a TV clip of a grandmother showing mementos of her rich and loving family life. She pointed to a photo of one of her granddaughters on the credenza but told the announcer she couldn't display the one of her granddaughter's wedding. When asked why, she reached in the drawer and pulled out the wedding picture. Her granddaughter had married a black man and she had a hard time dealing with that. She loved her grandchildren, she loved her granddaughter and said her grandson-in-law had always been very kind to her, but she still had difficulty accepting their interracial marriage. I was surprised that in the year 2004 that kind of thinking still existed, but I gave her every right to her opinion. To her credit, there was no bitterness or hatred in her voice, she simply had a hard time accepting something she wasn't used to.

The announcer finished the clip with a great quote – one that can help all of us better understand the process of ridding ourselves and our society of fear and prejudice. He said, "First comes tolerance, then acceptance, then irrelevance."

I reflect on so many things in our society that have taken that route. Jackie Robinson was the first black person to play major league baseball. He went through living hell, having to stay in a hotel separate from his white teammates, having his life threatened, being booed just for being black, but he broke the barrier. Soon our society began to tolerate black people being included in professional and major college athletics, then we began to accept it, and now it's not an issue – it's totally irrelevant.

Because of the Susan B. Anthonys of the world, women were granted the right to vote and hold office. At first we grudgingly tolerated it, then we accepted it, and now we don't even debate it – it's totally irrelevant.

I remember when women teachers were paid less than men. After all, for married women it was a second income. Men were the "breadwinners." If a women wasn't married, she didn't need as much as the men raising their families. There was huge debate but eventually attitudes changed and men and women were placed on the same salary schedule. At first it was tolerated, then accepted, and now it's irrelevant.

In 1948, Senator Hubert Humphrey made an

emotional speech at the Democratic National Convention favoring civil rights for African Americans. At that time it was considered political suicide to wage such a campaign, but now open discussions about issues of race are commonplace. In 1957, the National Guard had to be called out to escort James Merideth, their first African American student, onto the campus of Ole Miss. Eventually black students were tolerated on Southern campuses, then their right to a college education was accepted, now it's irrelevant. Admittedly we have a long way to go in terms of race relations, but we have made great strides in the past 60 years and we need to give ourselves some credit for our progress. Who knows, maybe someday a person's race will be irrelevant. Wouldn't that be wonderful? And just think how much happier and harmonious our lives will be.

In 1952 and 1956, Adlai Stevenson ran for President against Dwight Eisenhower. A major question arose about Stevenson's ability to govern because he was a divorcee. Divorce was once taboo, then we began to tolerate it, then we accepted it, and now a person's marital status is not a consideration in his or her employability, political stature, morality or holiness in the eyes of God. It's irrelevant.

Looking back at history, only 40 to 50 years ago we were in the dark ages on some of these issues. Perhaps 40 to 50 years from now we may look back and wonder what all of the debate over sexual orientation was all about.

But for now, it is a real issue so let's look at it, discuss it, debate it, and see if we can get to a time when whether a person is "gay" or "straight" is not an issue – when *everyone* has the right to be free of discrimination and harassment on the job, when *everyone* has the right to enter into a loving relationship, when *everyone* has the right to his or her sexuality, regardless of sexual orientation. Let's see if we can get to a time when fear and judgment about sexual orientation moves to tolerance, then acceptance, then irrelevance. Then comes the best part – love, peace and harmony – the natural order of things.

"LOVE, PEACE, AND HARMONY ARE THE NATURAL ORDER OF THINGS."

Chapter Three

The
Fundamental
Question:

"Choice or Chance?"

The Fundamental Question: "Choice or Chance?"

When my wife's grandmother, Rose, was a little girl, she was left-handed. Trying to change her so she could be like the "normal" right handed children, teachers would ridicule her and hit her left hand with a ruler when she tried to write. Why would any adult do that to a child? The answer is simple. They thought being left-handed was a choice and they were going to correct her stubborn ways so she could be like all of the "normal" children. Although their intentions were good, they didn't stop to think that God had created her left-handed. But neither physical nor verbal nor emotional abuse could change her. When I met Rose, she was in her 70s and still left-handed. That's the way God created her and that's the way she stayed. Nothing the well-meaning adults did to torment her could alter God's plan for her to be a south paw. Most of us agree that being right or left-handed is not a choice. We don't question God's motives, we don't think God made a mistake, we don't think that some evil force is behind left handedness, we just accept lefties the way they are. They might be in the small minority, but they're perfectly normal. We went from tolerance to acceptance to irrelevance. Could we possibly do the same with sexual orientation someday?

How did you make your choice?

So there you were, back in 4th or 5th grade, just starting to experience your sexuality. If you are male, you probably experienced erections, perhaps a few nocturnal emissions (wet dreams), and maybe even your first experience with a powerful "climax" through masturbation. If you are female, maybe you felt clitoral sensations, maybe you felt tingly when that cute boy walked by, maybe you even experienced an orgasm or two. It was pleasant and powerful and at the same time strange and scary. As great as everything felt, some guilt feelings accompanied the pleasure. There were so many questions, so many emotions, and so much confusion. Was that when you first made your "choice" to be hetero or homosexual? You might be thinking, *"It never even occurred to me that I had a choice. It just happened."* Listen to what you just said. Most people would respond in this way, even those who spew the most distasteful remarks at the anti-gay rallies.

So the fundamental question seems to be this: Is sexual orientation a *choice* or is a person *created* "gay" or "straight"? Since most homosexuals believe that it's not a choice and most people who think that it is a choice are heterosexual, the questions in this chapter are mostly aimed at the "straights." If you honestly think it's a choice, you could be led to criticize and even ridicule homosexual behavior. If after reflecting on the queries in this chapter, however, you believe that a person is created with his or her sexual orientation, you may be on your way to becoming less judging and more loving.

As much as I used to get angry with the hate-filled letters to the editor and the cold, cutting, insensitive remarks at the anti-gay rallies, I am going to try to keep an even emotional keel as I pose these challenges. I hope you take some time to calmly reflect upon them.

You may find, as I did, that you could not begin to understand another's sexual orientation. Most straight people cannot identify with the attractions or desires of gay people. Perhaps a gay person cannot identify with the sexual desires of a straight person. But by examining how your own sexual orientation came about, maybe you will conclude that another's came about in the same way.

You may feel strongly that you "preferred" to be straight and that gays being attracted to the same sex is a "preference" as well. You may feel that you "chose" to be straight, just as gays

31

"choose" to be gay. Whether one chooses his or her sexual orientation is perhaps at the heart of the debate. It is not the purpose of this book to argue with anybody, but rather to ask that you take time to reflect upon how you came about deciding your sexual "preference". Maybe you'll discover it's not a "preference" at all.

For those who believe sexual orientation is a choice, listen to your inner dialogue as you ponder these questions.

How did you choose to be heterosexual? Did you weigh your options and decide to be straight? Did you read books or watch videos or have discussions with others to explore your options?

When did you choose to be heterosexual? Was it in grade school, or junior high, or high school or were you in college at the time? Did you ever vacillate between being heterosexual and homosexual? Did you experiment both ways and then make your decision?

Was your heterosexuality something you *learned*? If so, who *taught* it to you? Was it your parents or teachers or siblings or perhaps a minister. If someone did teach you, *how* did they teach you? Did they give you a lecture about the fact that you should feel all tingly about the opposite sex but not someone of the same sex? Did they show you movies about how to get aroused by the opposite sex? Did they show you pictures of both boys and girls and teach you which one should get your hormones raging?

You may be thinking, "This guy is absolutely nuts. They may have taught me some things about sex but they didn't teach me *how* to be attracted to the opposite sex – they didn't even talk about it. It just happened naturally. That's the way God made me." Listen to what you just said. If your sexual orientation came about naturally because that's the way God made *you*, wouldn't it be possible that a gay person's sexual orientation came about in the same way?

Let me pose another question about choice. If it was a choice for you, when did you realize that you had that choice? The word "choice" would indicate that you had sexual feelings both ways – you liked boys *and* you liked girls – but decided that your choice would be people of the opposite sex. If you think about it, your sexual orientation may not have really been a choice at all – *it probably just happened*. Maybe your family didn't convince you to be straight after all, maybe you just *inherited* straight genes. Maybe your religious leaders didn't teach you to prefer people of the opposite gender, maybe you just naturally gravitated towards them. You probably didn't choose at all. Do you suppose the same could be true of a gay person?

Next question: *Why* did you choose to be straight? Was it on moral grounds? Was it because of your religious upbringing? Was it just because you are a holy person? Was it to

33

please your family and abide by their values? Was it societal pressure? Was it to avoid ridicule and harassment if you didn't conform to society's code? Or did you "choose" to be heterosexual because it just came about naturally, in which case it doesn't seem like it was really a choice, does it?

One of the most convincing testimonies in the debate about choice came from a gay priest in the mid 1980s. You can imagine the controversy an openly gay priest would cause in a conservative community. The battle of words was a bitter one with some of the most blistering, hate-filled remarks coming from some of the most "religious" people. In an article in the local newspaper addressing the issue of choice the priest remarked, "There is no way a person would go through this living hell if he or she had a choice." Please keep in mind that the "living hell" he was referring to was not his homosexuality, but the hatred, hurt, judgment and ridicule he had to endure because of it. Given the choice, he would have gladly succumbed to the wishes of society and become heterosexual, *but he didn't have that choice.* He wasn't as lucky as those who condemned him – those God created heterosexual.

If you honestly believe that you made a conscious choice to be straight because of your sound moral character and your devotion to God and everything good, so be it. If you feel that gives you the right (or even the duty) to condemn those who have "chosen" the gay lifestyle, feel free to condemn to your heart's content. But please refrain from the mean-spirited and hurtful gay-bashing we've heard so much of recently. Opposing homosexuality in a calm demeanor is one thing, bashing is another. And you may want to take some time each day to thank God for guiding you to be heterosexual.

If, however, you conclude that your heterosexuality just came to you in a natural, God-given manner – *without a choice;* maybe you could accept that homosexual people came about their sexuality in the same God-given manner as you – *without a choice.* You might not understand how, you might not understand why, but you might someday believe (as I do) that God *is* the One who created Adam and Steve just the way they are. And I don't know about you, but I'm not about to argue with God.

"It never
occurred to
me that I
had a choice.
It just
happened."

Chapter Four

Please, Don't Thump Your Bible

Please, Don't Thump Your Bible

I can't recall seeing any recent news stories about politicians attending anti-Jewish, anti-African American, anti-Native American, or anti-anybody rallies. We would not only say that such rallies are politically incorrect, we would wonder how any human could demean and criticize another person in such a manner. Some might even say such a rally would be "un-Christian." I haven't seen many church people conducting anti-divorce or anti-having-children-out-of-wedlock or anti-living-together before-you-get-married rallies. Yet-anti gay rallies are commonplace; complete with politicians and religious leaders using vicious, cutting remarks that tear at the very hearts of gay people and their families. Politicians who are so careful not to say anything that might offend minorities openly rip on homosexuals, thinking it's not only their right to do so but their responsibility. Attendees carrying placards with biblical quotes spew vehemently hateful rhetoric bashing gay people and, in their holiness, seem to be more than justified in doing so.

I recently read a synopsis of a poll and a comment that "many believe homosexuality is against God's will,'" caught my attention. The question I pose, and it is cause for discussion, is this: If God didn't will homosexuality, why did He create homosexuals? Some would say He didn't *create* people that way; it is their *choice*. So we're back to the fundamental question. Did God create Adam and Steve the way they are or did they choose to be gay. (Before you answer that, perhaps it would be worthwhile to reflect again on Chapter 3.)

As we continue to debate the issue, I do have one request. ***Please, don't thump your Bible.*** I have read so many hate-filled letters to the editor and have watched the news quips of those opposed to homosexuality quoting "the Bible" to support their claims. That's OK, but I have believed for a long time that most of us are selective Bible readers. People thump their Bibles and quote scripture with the best of them when they need to back their own opposition to gay people, but if they took the Bible literally (as they claim to) they would have to be opposed to lot of things that are common place in our society today, things they may even be "guilty" of themselves.

For example, they would be dead set against

divorce because the Bible clearly states its opposition to divorce many times over. In Matthew 19:9, we read, "And I tell you this, a man who divorces his wife and marries another commits adultery...." Mark 10:10 tells us that "Whoever divorces his wife and marries someone else commits adultery against her. And if a woman divorces her husband and remarries, she commits adultery." By the way, these words are straight from Jesus' mouth. Later Paul tells the Corinthians, (1 Corinthians 7:10), "Now for those who are married I have a command that comes not from me but from the Lord. A wife must not leave her husband and if she does leave him, let her remain single or else go back to him. And the husband must not leave his wife." There is little room for divorce if you interpret the Bible literally, yet we hear no opposition to it from the pulpit. From those same pulpits, however, we do hear opposition to homosexuality because "it's in the Bible." If you oppose homosexuality for biblical reasons and the Bible is your ultimate source of truth, why do you not oppose divorce on those same grounds?

It is common place today to have women active in our churches, many of them leading the charge against homosexuality and quoting the Good Book as their source. Thousands of Christian churches are thriving under the leadership of their women ministers. But the Bible clearly opposes this. Again, Paul (1 Corinthians

15:34) states that "Women should sit silent during church meetings. It is not proper for them to speak. They should be submissive, just as the law says. If they have any questions to ask, let them ask their husbands at home, for it is improper to speak at church meetings." In 1 Corinthians 11:5, we read "A woman dishonors her husband if she prays or prophesizes without a covering on her head. If she refuses to wear a head covering she should cut off all of her hair." Sounds kind of outdated doesn't it? But, hey, it's in the Bible.

Some of us remember the old marriage vows and the Bible verses that accompanied them stating that "A man is responsible to Christ, a woman is responsible to her husband...." (1 Corinthians 11:3). And we all (especially the men) remember the famous "Wives, be submissive to your husbands." All but the staunchest of conservatives would have a hard time with that one, and I would guess the National Organization of Women would not support a literal translation of the Bible on the issue of wives being submissive to their husbands.

So before you use verses from Deuteronomy or Leviticus to support your opposition to homosexuality, remember that those same books of the Bible prescribe that rebellious sons be taken to the town elders and led out of town to be stoned to death. (Boys didn't sass their parents much in those days.) Also consider that adultery and homosexuality are forbidden in the same sentence. Where? In the Bible.

If you're thinking "C'mon, the Bible was written years ago, times they are a changin' and things are different now – we can't take all that stuff literally." I rest my case.

Before we leave our discussion, I might suggest a verse or two for those who want to continue to spew judgment, bitterness, and even rage towards gays and their friends. Try reading Luke 18:9-14 and see if one of the characters sounds familiar.

Back to the Issue

Don't get me wrong. I'm not denying anyone's right to oppose homosexuality based on moral convictions. What I would suggest, though, is that you think before you speak, and that you honestly answer the questions raised in Chapter Three. Think about how hurtful your words may be before you engage in "gay bashing." Ask yourself if the gay person really has a choice. Go a step beyond that. Ask that even if he or she *does* have a choice, is it any business of yours? Is a gay couple doing anything to infringe on your rights? Are they taking something away from you? Are they hurting you in any way?

Reflect on all of God's creation. If God did not create homosexual men and women, then why did he create homosexuality in the animal kingdom? Biologists tell us that most animal species have the same percentage of homosexuals as humans. Did the animals choose their sexuality, or did God create them that way? Perhaps homosexuality is just as *natural* to homosexuals as heterosexuality is to heterosexuals. Maybe God made all of us just the way we are, and maybe that's OK.

Although you may never understand another's sexual orientation, you may begin to replace judgment and disdain with tolerance. From tolerance you begin to accept that God not only created Adam and Eve, He *also* created Adam and Steve – in His own image and likeness – just like you. Then you move beyond acceptance to the point where another's sexual orientation is totally irrelevant. You begin to behold that person as a marvelous child of God, just as you are a marvelous child of God. Then judging less and loving more manifests your boundless potential as a warm, accepting, caring human being. The sky is the limit.

"**M**AYBE **G**OD MADE ALL OF US JUST THE WAY WE ARE, AND MAYBE THAT'S **OK**."

Chapter Five

What is Natural?

What is Natural?

In our industrial arts classes back in junior high, we learned about the threading of nuts and bolts. "Rightsy tightsy, leftsy loosen." That's the way they were threaded. Except when it came time to change the blades in the table saw. The shaft and bolts were threaded the other way. It just wasn't "natural" like the others. There was a good reason for the saw to be threaded "backwards." If it were threaded "naturally," the blade could loosen as the saw turned and send the blade flying. (Many would consider that a safety hazard.) Although it seemed strange to turn everything in the opposite direction, we just accepted the reality and turned the nut the way it was threaded. Most of us didn't understand or even care why the designing engineer had the foresight to thread everything "unnaturally" and in reverse, we just trusted his or her judgment.

The couplings connecting the tank to many

propane gas grills are threaded in reverse. It's uncomfortable to turn everything opposite of what seems "natural," but I never questioned the engineer who designed the gadgetry.

So many of those who criticize gays on religious grounds say that heterosexuality is "natural" and is in line with God's plan and that homosexuality is "unnatural" and therefore against God's will. I marvel at their insight but wonder where they got privilege to knowing The Almighty's intentions. Do they have a direct line to God? Did they take classes to learn how to gain access to His will? Did God come to them in a dream? Do they know for certain what is "natural" and "unnatural" in God's great plan? Or are they just saying that something is God's will because it seems comfortable to them, and therefore "natural." I didn't claim to know the wisdom or intentions of the engineer who designed the threads on the table saw and I don't claim to know the wisdom or intentions of the One Engineer who designed all of us. I *think* God made all of us, including Adam and Steve, just the way we are. I *think* God determined our sexual orientation and that he loves us all equally. I don't *think* God condemns homosexuals and I don't *think* He would excommunicate them from His church. But I'm not going to sit here and tell you for sure that I *know* when it comes to interpreting the will of God. I'm not that smart and I'm not that arrogant.

If you are still undecided on the "natural vs.

unnatural" thing, look back at the debate over birth control just a few decades ago. Those who opposed birth control except the rhythm method argued that to use anything else was in violation of God's "natural" plan. One of two things has to happen here. Either you agree with them because they have the same access to God's will as you, or you disagree with them because their information about God's plan is off base with yours. Do you suppose that neither really has such an open channel to God that you can interpret His will for the rest of us?

How About a Little Levity and Some "Wisdom from Grandpa Schwartz"

Although I'll embellish the story a bit, it is basically true and Grandpa Schwartz's quote is real. Besides, it ties in perfectly with this chapter. A friend told of the time his cousin came out of the closet at a family gathering. Try to imagine the mixture of responses. Picture a couple of the aunties gasping and immediately going into prayer. Some may have been shocked. Others may have said they suspected it all along. Maybe Mom was crying, not because her son was gay but because she knew the cruelty he would face and the hurt he would have to endure. Dad probably said, "Don't worry, Honey, he's a strong person, he knows who he is, he's confident and he'll be just fine."

But Grandpa Schwartz so humorously put it all in perspective as he placed his hands behind his head, leaned back and said, "Well, ya gotta screw the way you're threaded." Grandpa Schwartz provided a little levity along with some great insight. Here was a man of grandfatherly age who was totally open and accepting of what to him was "natural" for his grandson. It didn't shake him a bit. His grandson was fine, thank you, just the way he was.

"Ya gotta screw the way you're threaded."

Grandpa Schwartz

Chapter Six

Why the Bashing?

Why the Bashing?

A group of people were socializing around the company conference table. One of the guys in the group, seeing all white people and thinking he was safe, proceeded to tell a racist joke. (Of course, a racist joke is never appropriate and should never be considered "safe.") What he didn't realize was that one of the women in the group had adopted an African American child. She was his mother. It was a tense and embarrassing situation to say the least. The mother was hurt and angry, the joke teller was flustered to tears and apologetic as he could be, and everyone else in the room was uncomfortable as well. The one who told the joke never would have considered doing so had he known about the woman's adopted son. He would have done anything to take back his words, but it was too late. He had already caused pain to one of his co-workers; pain that would not easily go away.

Would he have said what he said had he known? Probably, not. Most people just would not do that. Yet many of those same people would think nothing of openly bashing gays and their families and do so under the guise of religion or moral righteousness. To calmly discuss the issue is one thing, to bash is another.

A recent political gathering on the issue of gay marriage drew a considerable crowd of people from both sides. A newspaper account of one woman's experience was both upsetting and heartwarming. The article included a picture of her family when the kids were small, then went on to explain that one of the sons, now in his early twenties, is gay. The mother said that their son informed them in junior high of his sexual orientation. They were a close knit church-going family with strong religious beliefs. They totally accepted, supported, and unconditionally loved their son just the way he was; the way God created him. Then she went on to tell of the cutting, hateful remarks that she had to endure from the people on the other side. One woman, face filled with vehemence, told her that her son was a sinner and was going to Hell. She told the mother that she was wrong and a sinner to support her own son.

Can you imagine that? This is the same person who probably teaches children in Sunday school that God loves them unconditionally, and then openly condemns a mother and her son. What gave her the right to tell another, a total stranger, that her child is a sinner and destined to eternal damnation just because he is gay? Is there any religious doctrine that would condone such behavior? Yet it is allowed to go on because the remarks are made against a gay person, and a gay person deserves it, right? After all, gays choose to be gay. In her heart of hearts, does the tormentor really believe that people choose to be gay? Does she really think that *her* God is going to condemn someone else because he or she is homosexual? Why the bashing? Why the misunderstanding? Why the hatred? Why the judgment? Why the condemnation? Why? Why? Why?

Do gay bashers think people choose their height? Do they think people choose their skin color? Then why do they think a person chooses sexual orientation? Would they openly criticize or ridicule another for being too short or too tall or because they have blue eyes? Probably not – yet they flaunt their disdain for homosexuals. Even if they believe sexual orientation is *not* a choice, why wouldn't they afford gay people the same sensitivity they would offer to others?

Even if some believe that sexual orientation *is* a choice, why do they have to publicly condemn and chastise others? Are they the world's leading religionists? Are they noted moralists with the inside scoop on God's word and will? Let me emphasize that we all have every right to our own opinions and we should discuss and debate them openly, but I question the wisdom and motives of anyone who spews hatred and bitterness or makes fun of another's sexual orientation, whether he or she believes it's a choice or not.

Can't we replace the judgment and name calling with love and acceptance – or at least tolerance? Can't we replace the flaming rhetoric with some calm and intelligent discussion? Can't we replace our fear with faith in the idea that maybe we can all live side by side and do so very happily? Nobody is going to have to lower their standard of living or have a diminished relationship with his or her spouse or partner just because there happens to be a gay couple living next door. It *is* quite possible for gays and straights to peacefully coexist – really it is!

If you're one who regularly or occasionally gets involved in gay bashing, be careful. Your words may embarrass you. Much like the person who told the racial joke at the office, your words could offend or even deeply wound someone else – and they could come back to haunt you. You could be hurting a close friend and not even know it. And keep this in mind. Your bashing may say more about you than it does about the people you bash.

"THEY WERE A CLOSE KNIT CHURCH GOING FAMILY WITH STRONG RELIGIOUS BELIEFS. THEY TOTALLY ACCEPTED, SUPPORTED, AND UNCONDITIONALLY LOVED THEIR SON JUST THE WAY HE WAS; THE WAY GOD CREATED HIM."

Chapter Seven

The Sacred Institution

The Sacred Institution

According to one survey, 55% of those polled agreed with the statement that "if gays are allowed to marry, the institution of marriage will be degraded." Let's take a walk down memory lane to the 1950s – back to the "good old days" when divorce was rare and considered a little taboo. Some churches wouldn't let people be a part of their flock if they were divorced, especially if they remarried. Very few people lived together without being married because cohabitation was considered by most to be sinful. Few children were born out of wedlock and the teenage pregnancy rate was a fraction of what it is today. Marriage was entered into very seriously because it was meant to be a lifetime commitment, and pre-marital sex was less prevalent than it is today. (At least it wasn't as open.)

The institution of marriage has changed greatly in the past 60 years or so. Today nearly fifty percent of marriages end in divorce. Couples, young and old, living together without the formality of marriage is commonplace. (Back in the days when it was judged as unholy and unacceptable it was called "shacking up.") It is not uncommon today to hear of a man fathering three children with three different women without being married to any of them and often with little or no intention to provide for them. Just as common are women having three children by three different fathers without being married. Couples enter into marriage very nonchalantly saying, "We'll try it and if it doesn't work out we can always get a divorce." But we all know the *real* threat to the institution of marriage is homosexuality. If gays are allowed to marry, marriage would no longer be "sacred" like it is now.

Just for the fun of it, here is a list of some possible hazards to the institution of marriage. Take a minute or two to rank them from the most to the least serious threat.

❖ Infidelity (More commonly referred to as "cheating")

❖ Divorce

❖ Physical, emotional, or verbal abuse of spouse

❖ Physical, emotional, or verbal abuse of children

❖ Financial problems

❖ Losing attraction for each other

❖ Couples living together without being married

❖ Having children out of wedlock, especially with multiple partners

❖ Alcohol or drug abuse

❖ Gays being allowed to marry

I think we can safely say that there are probably a lot more serious threats to "the institution" than gays being allowed to marry. Keep in mind here, we're not trying to make moral judgements about any of the above behaviors but do pose these questions: If you *are* morally opposed to gay marriage and consider it a threat to the sacredness of marriage, how could you *not* be opposed to divorce or cohabitation or having children out of wedlock with multiple partners, on the same grounds? Or to word it another way, if you are *not* opposed to the items on the above list and don't think the government should ban such things as divorce, cohabitation or having children out of wedlock with multiple partners; how could you *possibly* be in favor of a constitutional ban on gay marriages? People may have a lot of reasons for their opposition to gay rights, but the idea that it is a threat to the institution of marriage seems pretty weak when compared to some of the other perils it faces today.

Some may feel squeamish about one or more of the items on the list because it hits a little close to home. They might say, "Quit judging my behavior and mind your own business. What I do with my life is up to me." I couldn't agree more. Perhaps we could do the same for gay people?

There's an old song that proclaims, "The old gray mare she ain't what she used to be, many long years ago." Well, the institution of marriage maybe ain't what it used to be either, but I don't think we can blame it on homosexual people. Giving gay couples the right, respect, and recognition to live in a loving, committed relationship shouldn't be a threat to anyone's individual marriage nor should it pose any threat to the "institution" itself. What are we fearing?

Homosexuality and the Family

There are those who fear that homosexuality is a threat to the "family" and "family values." I have news for you. Homosexuals are already in families and have some pretty strong family values. They are sons and daughters, brothers and sisters, nephews and nieces, aunts and uncles, and parents and grandparents. Although some families disown some of their members for being gay, it doesn't change most families love and commitment one iota. Not only do most parents accept their son or daughter, I am guessing that most accept their gay son's or daughter's partner just as they would their straight son's or daughter's husband or wife. They love them all and are pleased to see them happy together.

If you're fearful of gays being a threat to the family, just look around and observe the strong and loving families of most gay people. You can put your fears to rest.

"GIVING GAY COUPLES THE RIGHT, RESPECT, AND RECOGNITION TO LIVE IN A LOVING, COMMITTED RELATION-SHIP SHOULDN'T BE A THREAT TO ANYONE'S INDIVIDUAL MARRIAGE NOR SHOULD IT POSE ANY THREAT TO THE 'INSTITUTION' ITSELF."

Chapter Eight

Is Marriage Just a Piece of Paper?

Is Marriage Just a Piece of Paper?

In the late 1960s and early 1970s, the sexual revolution had hit full steam and many, especially college students, were questioning the institution of marriage. I remember them saying "Marriage is just a piece of paper." With some modification, an examination of their statement might have merit. Although marriage itself may be more than just a piece of paper, the marriage *license* is indeed just that – a piece of paper. It's an important piece because it affords married couples the civil rights the union offers such as property inheritance, tax filing status, family health insurance benefits, etc. The license itself doesn't go far beyond that. A building permit gives the builder permission to build a house but it doesn't build the house. The builder has to do that. So it is with the marriage license. It gives the people the right to enter into their life-long relationship, but it does nothing to actually build the marriage – that's up to the two involved. As one minister said to newlyweds at the close of their marriage ceremony, "The wedding is over. Now it's time to build a marriage."

Let's explore three levels of the institution as we know it today. First is the legal aspect which includes the marriage license and all of the civil rights that accompany it. Then there is the ceremony, which can be either a religious ceremony performed by the clergy or a civil ceremony performed by a justice of the peace or other public authority. The religious wedding performed in a church, masque, synagogue or other holy building recognizes the couple being joined by God. Some couples take the religious part very seriously and others are less than serious about it, having the church wedding more to please the family than anything else. Then there's the deepest part of the whole thing, the real love and the real commitment, the part of the union that rises to the spiritual level. This is the one that really *binds* the relationship; the one that gets the couples through the highs and lows of a lifetime together – the physical challenges, the financial hardships, the hurts and heartbreaks, the love pats and love spats, the joys and successes, and everything in between. This is what the "marriage" is really all about, whether it was a religious ceremony or not. This is the one that really matters. The paper we call the license may be the official recognition of the marriage, but it is not the marriage anymore than the building permit is the building.

Let's examine what the marriage license does offer. It does guarantee the civil rights that we've mentioned and it does give official recognition to the union.

Does it give people the right to live together? Yes. But tens of thousands of couples are living together *without* being married. I'm guessing that most couples today live together before they get married, and some have children before they decide to officially tie the knot.

Does it give them the right to enjoy sex with each other? Yes. But we couldn't even begin to count for the number of sexual encounters outside of marriage.

Does it give them the right to be committed in a monogamous relationship? Yes. But many live in fidelity even though they are not officially married.

Does it give them the right to experience deep love and to be there for each other through thick and thin? Yes. But many do that without the bonds of matrimony and many who professed their marriage vows at the alter divorce at the drop of a hat.

So let's conclude that a marriage is not the license or the ceremony or the solemnity of the vows, but the long lasting commitment that follows. Although sex is a big part of most marriages, sex is not the only thing that makes a lifetime commitment endure. Although married couples enjoy some advantages under the law, it is not the civil amenities that hold marriages together. What really makes it all worthwhile is the lasting love, the long walks and talks, navigating the peaks and valleys together, the joy of building a life together, that "indescribable something" that only happily committed couples can experience.

So I have to ask this question, especially of those opposed to gay "marriages" or "civil unions" or whatever you want to call them. Why do you want to deny these deeply spiritual aspects of a relationship to people just because they are gay? Don't they have the right to live and love and laugh together just like you? Don't they have the right to enjoy their intimacy just like you? Don't they have the right under God to have someone to love them and be there when they hurt, just like you? Don't they have the right under God to build their lives together, to plan their home together and to go through their highs and lows together, just like you? Don't they have the right under God to the same civil advantages as you? If not, why not?

Two arguments that we've already discussed seem to surface, but let's revisit them. First is the religious argument. Keep in mind that although many are opposed to gay marriage based on their religious beliefs, almost as many religious leaders and lay people are perfectly OK with it, religiously speaking. So does anyone have the right to impose their religious beliefs on others? The second argument, and to me the weakest, is that it is a threat to the "sacredness" of marriage. To echo our thoughts from an earlier chapter, with divorce, cohabitation, children being born out of wedlock, spousal abuse, infidelity, etc. so prevalent in our society today; how can two gay people living in love and harmony pose as much of a threat to the institution as these things. To those who think that a gay union is a threat to their own marriage, I would have to be quite candid and question the strength of your relationship. How could a gay couple living and loving together possibly be a threat to a strong marriage?

If, on the other hand, your relationship brings you joy and happiness; why would you want to deny others the right to share that same kind of joy and happiness just because they're gay? It may seem a little (or even a lot) uncomfortable at first, but what have you got to lose?

Maybe I Can Answer That

Do you recall the story in an earlier chapter about the woman who just couldn't deal with her granddaughter's marriage to an African American? What did she lose by not accepting him? She didn't lose her granddaughter's love, her granddaughter loved her anyway. She did not lose the love and kindness of her African

American grandson-in-law. He treated her with kindness anyway? What she did lose was her own chance to be loving and accepting. Her bitterness and mistrust decreased the flow of the Divine love that could have been pouring through her in abundance. Her granddaughter and grandson-in-law were probably a little hurt, but they rose above it. The one who really lost out was the grandmother. Isn't that sad?

One of my favorite TV shows had a scene that involved a man seeing one of his high school friends for the first time in years. His friend had become a transexual. He was shocked at first but decided to meet his old chum for lunch. While discussing the situation with his coworker, he told of his grandmother's lesson on the difference between being open and closed-minded. She said, "To be closed-minded is to judge others and shut yourself off from an All-loving God." That's what judgment does. Doesn't it seem strange that some deep *spiritual* reflection might help us to accept gay people rather than to chastise them? Maybe as we really reflect on the fact that we didn't choose our sexual orientation but it is a God given trait, we would judge gay people less and accept them more. Maybe if we really let go of our fear and replaced it with open-minded acceptance we could come to realize that gay couples love each other just as much as straight couples do. Maybe we could then give their relationship the honor and respect it deserves. We admire a man and woman who commit their lives to each other and who exemplify what love is all about. Why can't we give that same admiration and respect to two gay people who exemplify that same kind of love and commitment? If we break down the barriers of ignorance and fear and look deep within ourselves maybe we would realize that God is the one who created Adam and Steve, and He blesses their love just as He blesses yours. Then we could spend less time trying to monitor other peoples' relationships and spend more time improving our own. We could all love and let love and the world may be a better place because of it.

The marriage license is a piece of paper. The church or civil ceremony is the wedding. A lifetime of commitment, love and laughter is the marriage. Why can't we just give everyone the right to enjoy it?

"TO BE CLOSED-MINDED IS TO JUDGE OTHERS AND SHUT YOURSELF OFF FROM AN ALL-LOVING GOD."

Chapter Nine

Marriages or Unions: Everyone Can Have Their Rights

Marriages or Unions: Everyone Can Have Their Rights

The first amendment to the constitution gives us freedom of speech, religion, press, petition and assembly. The second amendment gives us the right to bear arms. The fifteenth amendment gave black men the right to vote. The nineteenth amendment gave women the right to vote. The 26th amendment gave 18-year-olds the right to vote. In fact, most of the constitution is designed to give people rights, not take them away. Yet there's a big stir in some states about a constitutional amendment to ban gay marriage. A constitutional ban on gay marriage does the opposite of what our precious founding document was meant to do – that is to grant each of us freedom to live life, enjoy liberty and pursue happiness.

The debate will be heated, but if everyone backs off and gives a little bit we could reach a compromise that everyone could live with. We could approach marriage much the same way we do divorce – by separation of church and state. Two people get married in a church ceremony. The marriage is recognized by both the church and the state and both bestow upon the couple all of the rights that go along with the union. The state honors Catholic, Lutheran, Methodist, Jewish, Muslim, marriages of any religion, and even marriages performed outside of church by a Justice of the Peace. People can go to Vegas and be joined in holy matrimony at a drive through and the marriage is recognized by the state. The state doesn't really care much about the religious part of the contract; their concern is the civil portion. In the old days, and maybe even yet today, some churches did not consider a person married if he or she got married by another denomination or a justice of the peace. The state totally accepted the union with all of the rights, responsibilities, and privileges; but the church did not and many times took away that person's right to go to communion or participate in other sacramental ceremonies. Both the church's and the state's reactions to the marriage ceremony should be looked upon as acceptable. One aspect of marriage has to do with the civil concerns such as property ownership, tax filing status, etc. The other has to do with peoples' religious beliefs. Both are important to church going people, but the state should not dictate the church's rules of marriage, nor should the church dictate the state's laws about civil matters.

There are some who think the separation of church and state on the subject of marriage will bring America to its knees. But we have had civil and religious difference in matters of marriage for centuries. If a married couple decides to get a divorce, they go through our legal system and the divorce is decreed. In most cases they don't go through a church ceremony to get "unmarried." They simply satisfy the civil aspect of the law, become divorced and according to state and federal law are free to remarry. In some religions, however, the divorce is not recognized and the couple can not remarry and continue to receive communion or other sacraments. It is against church law.

Both are OK. The state can issue the divorce but the church doesn't have to recognize it. The church has every right to excommunicate divorcees who remarry and should be free of civil law that would force them to grant membership to the people who have violated church doctrine. Maybe people don't agree with the church's stand, maybe they are offended and terribly hurt by the church's response, but the church should have the right to set its own rules without interference from the state.

The point is this: We already have a working model of religious "marriage and un-marriage" coupled with "civil unions" (Vegas drive through) and "civil un-unions" (divorce decreed by the state). Why can't we have the same working model for marriages and civil unions for both straight and gay couples?

Here's the compromise that could make it happen

There will be discussion and debate but if everyone is willing to give a little, we arrive at a solution that should keep everyone happy. Start with the premise of a civil union available to all couples, gay or straight. With that union comes all of the civil benefits such as tax filing status, estate inheritance, health insurance and other spousal benefits. If an American marries a person from another country, the same laws of citizenship apply to the partner whether the union is between a man and woman or a same-sex couple. Let's not, for now at least, get hung up on what we call it. All people are allowed to unite as a couple and commit their love and life to each other and to be recognized by the state with all of the rights and privileges.

Now what about the marriage bit? We could leave that up to the churches. If churches want to recognize a gay union as a "marriage" they could do so. If they do not believe that the gay union is recognized by God in their religion, they don't have to perform same-sex marriages. This preserves any church's right to follow their religious doctrine as they see fit. Some will perform same-sex marriages and some won't, and both should be considered to be within the law. The people most important –

family and friends – will consider the couple "married" immediately and automatically, regardless of what it is called. Some churches will perform a religious ceremony for gay couples and welcome them into their fold. Others won't. Some churches might even excommunicate gay couples. Others won't. So go to the church that accepts you and your partner as you are and recognizes the spiritual aspects of your sacred union. It will be only a matter of time before we recognize and respect all relationships for what they are; a commitment to a lifetime of love and fidelity.

Maybe neither side is totally happy with the above suggestions, but if both sides would give a little, we can get past the tension and name calling and get on with the business of living in peace and harmony. We could all enjoy more freedom.

Those opposed to gay marriage can get rid of their fear. A gay marriage is not going to be a threat to your marriage. If you think gays having a ceremony to profess their lifelong commitment to each other is a threat to your relationship, maybe your relationship is in trouble already. If your marriage is solid, how could a gay couple's love for each other be a threat to your relationship or to the institution of marriage? If your marriage is solid, how could a gay couple achieving their dream of home ownership be a threat to you or your home ownership? If your marriage is solid, how would giving a gay couple the right to pass on their estate to their partner be a threat to you and your spouse? If your marriage is solid, how would a gay couple being covered by a health insurance policy affect you? If your marriage is solid, how could a gay couple having the same citizenship privileges as a man and woman affect you? If your marriage is solid and your job performance is up to speed, how could a law forbidding a company to fire an employee simply because he or she is gay affect your marriage or your employment? When you get right down to it, homosexuals being allowed to live and love together doesn't really hurt any of us, does it? Granting the right to gay couples to marry does not in any way infringe on the rights of anyone else, does it? So if gay marriage doesn't hurt anyone and does not take away anyone's rights, why do we need a constitutional amendment to ban it?

Chapter Ten

Overcome the Fear

Overcome the Fear

I'm going to borrow the title of a great book, *Love is Letting Go of Fear*, by Dr. Jerald Jampolsky. Perhaps by trying to understand more about another person's sexual orientation you may not learn to love that person, but maybe you can at least tolerate, or accept, or even make his or her sexual orientation irrelevant in your life. You may find what people do in their private lives doesn't detract from your freedom or standard of living or even your relationship with your partner. If you're married, you may find that gays have much less effect on your marriage and your family than your own actions towards your spouse and kids. You may find that the only effect another's sexual orientation has on your life is how you choose to let it worry you. You may find that if you are less concerned about another person's relationship you will be able to devote more time and energy making yours better. You may find that by judging less you can love more.

Dispelling the Myths

This chapter, like Chapter 3, is written in a style that addresses the fears of heterosexuals but certainly can be food for thought for all of us. It seems to me that so much of the hatred, fear and judgment of gay people comes from misunderstanding – specifically misunderstanding on three issues. If we could dispel the myths and foster deeper understanding, perhaps we could replace hatred and judgment with love and acceptance. We've already discussed all three issues, but let's revisit them and try to replace emotion with logic.

Myth number one is that gays choose their sexual orientation. We have discussed this one to death but ask yourself once again if you think a gay person announced to his or her family, "Oh, by the way Mom and Dad, I've decided I want to become homosexual." Or did you at one time tell your family and friends, "I've been giving this a lot of thought lately and I've decided that I am going to be heterosexual."

If you have come to the realization that sexual orientation is not a choice but an inherent trait, you are ready to move to the next level – that is to accept gay people as creations of the same loving God who created you. You were naturally endowed with attractions for people of the opposite sex just as homosexuals were naturally endowed with attractions to people of the same sex? Why? I don't know, I don't claim to know, and I don't need to know. I just accept it as it is.

Myth number two is that a relationship between two people of the same sex is merely sexual. This is no truer than to say that a marriage, or any committed relationship between a man and a woman, is purely sexual. Sex is a part of it, but a committed relationship goes far beyond the bedroom. It is holding hands, cuddling, sharing hopes and dreams together, going through the ups and downs together, building financial security together, laughing together, sharing good times with friends and family together, having spats and making up, becoming part of each others families, and all that other "stuff." When we attend a 25th or 40th or 50th anniversary party of a married couple we realize that their life together was a total commitment and a combination of all of the things in the sentence above. Why do we think that a committed relationship between a gay couple is any less? Because we've been taught to. We've been taught to think of a gay relationship as only a sexual attraction. But it's not. Most of us know of gay couples who have been together for years but we have rarely given them credit for the deep love they have for each other. We've never been taught to. We have never thought of a gay couple walking through a park as experiencing the same love for each other that a straight couple walking through the same park would be feeling. We've never been taught to. We have never thought that a gay couple sipping a glass of wine on their backyard deck, basking in the beautiful moonlight while marveling at the stars could experience the same romantic feelings as a straight couple in the same moonlight. We've never been taught to. We have never thought that a gay couple experiencing the death of one of the couple's parents could be feeling the same things that a straight couple would be feeling. We've never been taught to. We've never thought that a gay person watching his or her partner suffer a painful surgery would be going through the same things that a straight person would in that same situation. We've never been taught to.

This may be a good place to insert a tough question for the gay bashers at the rallies and the politicians who oppose gay rights. If after close examination of your inner thoughts you believe that sexual preference is not a choice, how could you possibly continue on the track you're on? How could you possibly continue to spew vehement disdain for gays and their families and do so under the guise of religion? How could you possibly continue a campaign to deny gay people the opportunity to enjoy all of the constitutional rights that others enjoy, including the right to spend their lives together in a recognized union? How could you possibly condemn them as sinners if that's the way God created them?

Isn't it time to change all that? Isn't it time to recognize the reality that sexual preference is inherent? Isn't it time to give gay people the right to commit their love to each other and to give them credit for doing so? All we have to do is do dispel the myths, get rid of the fear, and let love and empathy take over.

The third myth is the most puzzling. "If we allow gay couples to marry, it will take away the sanctity of marriage." I can understand the fear and emotion behind that argument, but I cannot understand the logic, especially in light of the discussion in Chapter 7. If we as a society want to specifically define marriage as a union between a man and a woman, I suppose it's something we all could live with. After all, it's simply a matter of semantics. But I have a hard time with society denying a gay couple the right to a committed union, whatever we want to call it, and to deny them the rights, respect and recognition that accompany it. That union would be *as* sacred, *less* sacred, or *more* sacred than any other marriage, depending upon the real strength of the respective relationships and the spiritual commitment of the people involved. We've discussed this before but let's echo some thoughts. The civil union (marriage license) gives *all* couples the legal rights they deserve, then each church denomination could determine their stand on homosexual marriage, and everyone could have the freedom to choose their church affiliations. Some churches would conduct same-sex marriages and some wouldn't and that should be fine with everyone. Every church should have the right to conduct or not conduct same-sex marriages as they see fit and every individual should have the right to choose his or her religious beliefs, spiritual path, and lasting relationships as long as it does not interfere with anyone else's right to do the same. Giving gay couples the same rights and recognition as a man and a woman doesn't deny *anyone's* right to life, liberty, and pursuit of happiness, including married people. Isn't it time to move beyond our hang ups and get on with the business of giving people freedom to live and love as they choose?

Moving From Fear To Love

Abraham Lincoln once said, "I don't like that man very much... I'm going to have to get to know him better." Man, what a philosophy! He didn't say, "I don't like that person. I wish he would change. Doesn't he know he's driving me up the wall?" He knew that if he could look beyond what made him uncomfortable he would see the good and, if not like the person, at least understand him better. So it is with any move from fear to love. If we can put aside judgment for a while and try to see things differently, we can change our whole way of thinking about something. When we change our thinking our attitudes change and when our attitudes change our behavior changes and when our behavior changes we get a whole new set of results. So it is with us individually and collectively changing our attitudes about homosexuality. If you look past a person's "gayness" and get to really know him or her, you'll probably find a very regular human being, with hopes and fears and joys and dreams similar to yours. You may find that in spite of the differences in your sexual orientation, you have a lot in common – you laugh, you cry, you feel joy, you feel pain, you have goals, you drive a car, you like some of the same people, you may dislike some of the same people, you have hobbies, etc. In fact, you might find that you're pretty much the same – both very normal human beings.

A long time ago a religious leader of his time said, "Judge not by appearances, but by righteous judgment." Using his advice I have learned to monitor my judgmental thoughts about someone or something and analyze them to see if they are consistent with my spiritual values and the kind of person I want to be. For example, if I make a mental judgment about a person's weight or dress or race or any such thing and recognize it for what it is – judging and unloving – I try to alter my thoughts immediately and see the person as the total miracle he or she is. When I'm successful at doing so, I find I'm trading unkindness and tension for love and harmony. That's a great trade!

We can do the same with our attitudes about gay relationships. Instead of chastising them for being gay, we could lovingly understand that their homosexuality is naturally inherited and determined by God. Instead of being uncomfortable with a gay relationship and seeing it as purely sexual, we could recognize the deep love that exists between the couple and admire their commitment to each other. Instead of thinking that a gay relationship is a threat to our own, we could recognize that any truly loving relationship creates harmony and understanding and makes the world a better place to live. Then soon we would accept gay marriage as we now accept other former taboos – like interracial marriage, interfaith marriages, remarriage after divorce, etc. We can then discover that having gay marriages exist in our society will be pretty much like the other former taboos – irrelevant.

"I DON'T LIKE
THAT MAN VERY
MUCH... I'M GOING
TO HAVE TO GET
TO KNOW HIM
BETTER."

ABRAHAM LINCOLN

Chapter Eleven

You're OK

You're OK

"Mom, Dad, I'm OK and there's nothing wrong with me." When I heard those words I knew everything was going to be all right. He was self-confident, self-directed, he knew who he was and where he was going.

Let me explain. Our three sons were home for a family get together one Sunday. The younger two left at the usual time but Kyle, our oldest, stayed on longer. After some small talk he asked if he could talk with us. We sat in the living room and he started by saying, "This is the hardest thing I've ever had to tell you so promise me you won't be upset." After we assured him that anything he wanted to talk about was OK, he said, "I'm gay." Although we were surprised and there were some tears, we were totally accepting and OK from minute number one. Let me interject that the tears were not because he is gay but rather for what he would have to endure because he is gay– the nasty letters to the editor, the hateful remarks from the sign totters at the rallies, the blistering sermons from the pulpit, the insensitive remarks of the politicians, the cutting remarks at parties, etc.

Our conversation was wonderful. In fact the whole experience was really neat. Pat and I both assured him that we were comfortable with everything and that our love for him was as strong or stronger than ever. It didn't affect us in any way. I remember saying, "That's the way God made you, and I'm not about to argue with God." You see, everything written in this book was well established in our minds long before we knew our son was gay. For years we viewed homosexuality not as a sinful choice, as some of the religionists would profess, but rather an inherited trait determined by God. We saw and acknowledged the long lasting-love and devotion in gay relationships that went far beyond sexuality. Our attitudes about sexual orientation had been well established long before our conversation that evening and our love for our sons had always been unconditional. We never missed a beat.

The thing that really put us at ease with everything was the quote at the beginning of the chapter. When Kyle said, "Mom, Dad, I'm OK and there's nothing wrong with me," any concern we may have had left. We knew he would be just fine and we knew that nothing in our relationships would change. I had always admired his strength and determination and that admiration deepens as I observe his competence and self-confidence overcoming the challenges he faces. Although our acceptance and support is important, nothing is as paramount as him knowing that he is OK with himself.

If I could convince gay men and women of just one thing it would be this: "You're OK and there's nothing wrong with you." Overcome your fears and doubts and accept yourself just the way you are. Don't let anyone talk you into thinking you are anything less than a loving, caring miracle created by an All Loving God to be just what you are. Don't let anyone talk you into believing that your life-long relationships are any less meaningful, less committed, or less dignified than any one else's. Don't let anyone talk you into believing that you are more or less in the eyes of God than anyone else. God created all of us to enjoy a life full of love and laughter and that does mean *all* of us.

Doesn't it seem strange that so much of what has been discussed in these chapters refers to Our Creator? It has been through quiet reflection on an All Loving God and religious teachings about love and acceptance that have prompted the ideas in this book. I had a hard time buying the idea that God would chastise and condemn people for their inherited sexual orientation. I had a hard time buying the idea that sexual orientation is a choice and found it frustrating when people would write and speak about God condemning people for "choosing" a gay lifestyle. And when I saw the guy holding the sign saying "God Created Adam and Eve, not Adam and Steve," I thought he was half right. God *did* create Adam and Eve, but someone *also* created Adam and Steve. I think the same God did both and I don't think He loves one more than the other. I might be called blasphemous by some, but it was in studying about God's unconditional love and in quiet spiritual reflection that I drew these conclusions.

To the parents of gay men and women I would say, "Your son or daughter is OK and there's nothing wrong with him or her." Neither is there anything wrong with you or the way you raised your family. If for some reason your son or daughter inherited gay genes, it was God's determination. I'm no preacher but I'm guessing His will is for you to totally accept and unconditionally love your children just the way they are. I'm also guessing that He would will for you to bless your son's or daughter's long term relationships just as you would bless your children's heterosexual relationships. Long term gay and straight commitments probably have more in common than differences. Families are families and the bonds of love don't ever have to be broken because of sexual orientation. And don't care what other people think. Be proud. In fact, be extremely proud that your family's love transcends what others do or say.

Let me interject another personal story here.

About ten months after Kyle talked to us, we were at an extended family picnic and he asked to go for a walk. He wanted to tell our other two sons and was wondering if I thought they would be OK with his being gay. I answered, "Absolutely. I don't think it will matter a bit to them." I was right. Neither of them batted an eye and it has been so gratifying to see them grow closer and closer as the years progress. I thank God often for instilling in all three of our boys a spirit of love and acceptance. I thank Pat's family and her brother Paul for paving the way and showing us what family is all about. People who say that homosexuality is a threat to the family haven't observed the strength of families that face the challenges of dealing with the cruelty of homophobia. They're pretty strong.

To those who may be reading this thinking that it's not quite that easy I would say, "Maybe it isn't, but give it a try." Parent/child or sibling relationships could easily become strained when a gay person comes out of the closet. It could be shocking and upsetting. It could be traumatic. It could be very uncomfortable at first. But with a little time, a lot of love, and some really open communications families can be put back together. Keep in mind that these are your sons and daughters, your brothers and sisters or your mothers and fathers and you are meant to get along. Work first towards toler-ance, then acceptance, then irrelevance. Once you get to that point, love takes over and you're back in the flow. Remember, love, peace, and harmony are the *natural* order of things.

To those who have disowned a family member because he or she is gay, I strongly urge you to reconsider your position. One of my neighbors in the small town where I grew up disowned his son when he married a Native American girl. They lived in the same town but rarely spoke. The mother was robbed of a relationship with her son. They missed their grandchildren growing up just a few miles away from their house. They missed Christmas Eves together and Fourth of July picnics. They reconciled when the father was on his death bed, which was wonderful, but think of what they could have had. Don't settle for a death bed reconciliation when you could enjoy so much more – a life full of good times and happiness. It may seem uncomfortable at first but you'll get used to it. Realize that they didn't choose to be gay – but they are – so accept it. Rise above it. Embrace the opportunity to reach a level of love and understanding you never thought possible. It's not too late.

Let's Get On With It

It's time to stop reading and start doing. Let's see if we can go beyond the bashing and name calling and be more tolerant of our differences, as uncomfortable as it may be. Before we depart, let me echo the Socrates quote from

Chapter 1, "I cannot teach a person anything. I can only make them think." I don't expect you, nor would I want you, to agree with everything we've discussed. But I do hope you take time to reread and rethink the issues presented, especially the issue of choice. If sexual orientation is not a choice but is endowed at birth by Our Creator it may leave us with one conclusion.

God Did TOO Make Adam and Steve

"MOM, DAD, I'M OK AND THERE'S NOTHING WRONG WITH ME."